ABUNDANCE

10 Bible Proofs of God's Provision

Thank you both for always being so faithful

Rob Betts

ABUNDANCE
Ten Bible Proofs of God's Provision
ISBN 979-8-9870477-0-5

7620 Cross Mill Rd.
Paducah, KY 42001

Dedication

To my wife Sarah: I am grateful for your partnership in ministry and your love and support as we endeavor to follow God together. I love you. You're my best friend.

To my children Allie, Brady and Abbie Grace: We have covered a lot of ground together, and you were troopers even in the hard places. I am grateful for your sacrifice.

Richy, I'm so glad we brought you on the journey.

To my parents and my brother who were with me in the beginning and helped to shape me into who I am today: We have seen a lot of stuff and God has always proved himself faithful. I love you.

To Rev. Marvin and Leah Yoder: You have taught us to serve God with grace and you continue to be a wonderful example for us to follow. Pastor Yoder, you have been my dean, my mentor, my pastor, my teacher, and my friend. Thank you on all accounts.

Lastly, thank you to the Hagin Family for your teaching and example of excellence in ministry. You have helped to develop within me a lasting faith that has changed the course of my family forever. I thank God that He has led me to be part of the Rhema family preaching the uncompromised gospel of the Lord Jesus Christ.

Contents

Foreword

I was honored when my friend Rob asked me to write the foreword for his book, *Abundance: Ten Bible Proofs of God's Provision*. I have known Rob and his family for a number of years—where they have come from and where they are today. I have watched them learn how to base their life decisions on biblical truths and to see the fruit of their faith.

Rob's book will be a great blessing to you. First, it is based upon the timeless truths of the Bible which are relevant for every generation. Second, this book is further authenticated by stories of Rob and his family proving these biblical truths of God's abundant provision in their own lives.

Sadly, many people have not been taught about God's willingness to provide abundantly for them. These people live their lives not knowing what God has promised and remain uninformed about God's will for their lives. Rob's book will help people move beyond being ignorant of what God desires so they can begin to live in God's provision!

Some people work hard, endeavor to manage their assets well, and make plans for the best possible life for themselves and their families. But when they don't recognize that it is God who ultimately provides for them, it leads them into pride and arrogance, causing them to think what they have has come about by their own efforts. They need to discover the truths in this book, that God is the One who blesses humanity and provides for them abundantly so they can give Him glory for His blessings.

Other people are locked into wrong thinking about themselves, their past, and even their current circumstances. For them, the biblical truths in Rob's book will serve as a tool to break the chains of wrong thinking in their mind. It will change their outlook and expectations in life. It will change the way they believe, act, and speak about the possibilities that exist for them. And ultimately, they'll receive more of God's abundant provision and help other people in a greater way.

There is a great need for people to know the truth about God's abundant provision. My prayer is that you—the reader of this book—will come to realize all that God has planned for you, learn to receive all God has provided for you, and live to reflect all of God's goodness to those around you.

Rev. Marvin Yoder

Marvin Yoder Ministries

Preface

There are many reasons why someone would write a book. The thought of notoriety, the possibility of penning a best seller, a sense of accomplishment. I am sure these are all very fine reasons, but none of them really matter to me. I wrote this book in hopes that it would help someone. The possibility of others reading this book and gaining a greater degree of knowledge is sufficient enough reason to write. I remember one of my Bible college professors telling our class to write books. He said, "Guys, they will last longer than you do." His words stuck with me.

When I think of all the knowledge I have gained through books, I am grateful that someone shared what they knew so that it wasn't lost when they passed on. As ministers especially, I think it is vital that we share what we know. I have learned so much from teachers and ministers that have shared their knowledge with me over the years. If I know anything, I can honestly say like Sir Isaac Newton, "If I have seen further, it is by standing on the shoulders of giants."

I hope this book helps you go even further with God than I have.

Acknowledgements

There are a couple of things that, as a first-time author, I discovered in writing this book that had never really crossed my mind beforehand. The first was that I needed a great editor to help me convey my message. I am happy to have found that person in Mrs. Dagny Darnell. Thank you, Mrs. Dagny, for helping me to share the truths in this book in a way that is easily understood. You have a gift from the Lord that is evident in the work you produce, and I am grateful you said yes to this project.

The second thing I discovered is that in order to better appeal to others and perhaps allow a book to stand out, I needed a great cover. The great cover on this book is the creative work of a wonderful family friend, Mrs. Marla Rhine. Thank you, Mrs. Marla, for taking an abstract thought and making it into something beautiful. I am grateful you allowed us to reap the benefits of your gifting.

Introduction

I grew up in the shadow of a bridge. Growing up in a small southern Illinois town, I would frequently climb up on the subdivision sign just on the edge of our Section 8 housing neighborhood and look at that bridge in the distance. I can remember thinking how that bridge led to everything good in life.

And in a way, that was true. Because I lived in an area that is literally a food desert (no grocery store, gas station or other small business which typically breaks up the landscape), the bridge was the way to get to everything. All of the modern conveniences necessary to survive, groceries, clothing, fuel, the rest of the world, were all located across that bridge.

It's no wonder that the bridge became a symbol for a better future. In my mind, everything I wanted all seemed to be just on the other side of that bridge, and getting to the other side meant I could go anywhere.

I find it interesting that, looking back, I now realize that those moments so long ago, as I stared off into the distance, have helped shape me into the person that I am today. I was dreaming of a life with more.

I wanted more options, more enjoyment, more of everything I didn't have.

Before we go much further, I should probably mention that though my childhood had some downsides, it also contained a great deal of positives. Growing up in a small town has benefits including knowing everyone, neighborhood baseball games in the summer until dark, sled riding the local hill in the winter, bike riding, fishing, and camping. The purpose of me telling you my story is not so that you'll feel sorry for me, it's simply my observation about how childhood has many intersections, pathways, and influences, all of which significantly impact the people we are to become.

I grew up in a two-parent household, the second child of a union ironworker and a cake decorator. My brother only slightly older than me, provided an opportunity for me to learn from his mistakes and escape some of the childhood punishments often brought about by his ignorance of situations. Our family lived in a modest three-bedroom home in the neighborhood I previously mentioned. We were surrounded by other families attempting to squeak out a living in often similarly impoverished circumstances.

My dad was a genuinely decent human being who instilled in us the value of hard work. "I was butchering at fifteen years old," he would say, both with a good deal of pride and some disappointment that his own dad had required rent at such an early age.

Yet he still modeled that kind of hard work daily. I still recall all those mornings when, as I woke up and stretched and wiped the sleep from my eyes, I would hear the distant rumble of dad's old blue Ford as he pulled out of the neighborhood on his way to fill up the gas tank in preparation for a day filled with cutting wood.

Dad was also a kind man, and "hard but fair," as he put it. A quick wit only to be matched by a short fuse: that was my dad in a nutshell. But I loved him in spite of his flaws, and I counted him to be one of the best men in the neighborhood.

There was no work for dad in our area, so he would travel as a union ironworker all across the country in order to ensure that we had enough to meet our needs. Since many times there was no work, things could get pretty tight.

And we weren't alone. The town where I grew up still has a significant rate of poverty. The most recent statistics from the US Census Bureau declares the county I'm from as the most impoverished one in the entire state. Lack was part of life for most of us and was marked with reminders like having to eat commodity foods.

If you've never had the opportunity to eat commodity foods, then let me enlighten you. Commodities were a number of foods with generic government labels purchased by the federal government (to keep farmers going) and then redistributed to provide supplemental food sources for people in low-income areas. Every month, we'd all get blocks of cheese, powdered milk, rice, peanut butter, and oats.

It just so happened that three of those commodities—peanut butter, oats, and powdered milk—were the main ingredients in no-bake cookies. So whenever commodity day rolled around, at every house that I went to visit, my friends would offer me no-bake cookies. To this day, they are a treat I despise because they taste to me like poverty.

I only share this background information so it helps you understand how growing up in this type of environment helped shape my longing to live at a higher level of provision. Growing up, I wasn't always poor, but as the second child of a construction worker during an era where construction was, at best, a hit and miss occupation, I was *sometimes* poor and I didn't like it.

Today, I am no longer sometimes poor. The truths contained in this book have helped me to overcome a poverty mindset and live a life filled with God's provision.

ɔ without things. You told us in Your Word that you ·anted us to prosper—"

It was at this moment that down in my heart I eard these words: "*Where did I tell you that in my Vord?*"

I had no response. I couldn't tell God where He ad ever revealed in His Word that He wanted His peo-le to live in abundance. I stood there taking spiritual ıventory, thinking back to sermons I had heard over ıe years that spoke about God's provision, but I re-lized that *I* had never studied God's Word for myself ·garding His will for the provision I needed.

I still remember how, during that moment, again own in my heart I heard these words: "*Find ten places ı My Word that prove it is My will that My people ve in abundance.*" I knew immediately that God was ·ying to help me get to a place where I could stand in ıith in the area of His provision so that I could stop truggling to make ends meet.

In the coming pages, I am going to share with ou the ten places that I found. I know now that there re countless others, but these ten places have helped ıe to go to a new level of living, to break the genera-.onal mindset regarding God's provision that had held ıy family in poverty for years.

Introduction

I suppose everyone feels like they have a story to tell that might be interesting enough for someone else to read. In my case I chose to share, and I hope the things contained in this book help someone else find a new level of financial freedom based on truths found in the Word of God.

I used to reflect on my humble beginnings and sometimes felt like I had broken out of a modern-day caste system and was now living as part of a higher caste which I was never expected to belong to. I'm no actor, singer, or overnight success mind you, but I do consider my life a success in more practical ways.

I am the first in my family to have graduated from college, including graduate school. I am respected by my peers, considered a good friend who makes a decent living, and I associate with men and women of good reputation.

I have experienced a lot of things those who grew up in my community did not typically have the luxury of experiencing. I have dined with dignitaries, conducted meetings with political influencers, and met with many people the world might consider influential. Occupationally, I have done well and have had a significant amount of success, especially for someone with my background. I was a person who came from generationally-impoverished people raised in a generationally-impoverished community.

Since putting into practice the truths in this book however, I have experienced a good deal of personal and professional success. I have served as a high-level government employee, I been an executive director of communications for a community college, and I have been recognized by my peers at a state level for leading a team that experienced significant growth in enrollment for my institution at a time (the COVID-19 pandemic) when enrollment was on the decline. I have served as an adjunct professor of both Speech and Interpersonal Communications, I'm a husband and a father of three, a minister and a district director for ministers who are part of the organization in which I hold credentials. Despite the hardships of my upbringing, I can honestly say that at this point in my life, I do not lack for any good thing.

Although I have experienced much success, it is a result of the goodness of God and His help in putting together the principles I've outlined in this book. As much as I would like to take the credit for my success, it has been a result of a deliberate attempt to follow God's plan for my life and that is a decision that has definitely paid off. I am, at this point in my life, living a life of ABUNDANCE!

I understand that this subject has over the years divided many Christians onto one of two sides of the fence: those who believe God wants us to live a life of

full provision and others who are adamantl
to a gospel that includes any type of finan
ing. And I am not what some would call a
preacher, meaning abundance is not a teac
have spent much time sharing publicly. Ye
I have not really spoken on the subject ofte
with all my heart that God does want us to li
dance.

A number of years ago, my life could
scribed as successful. I was in a place in my
I couldn't afford to pay even my family's ba
sities like groceries, gas, and utilities. It see
was always coming up short. I would make it
it seemed like I was always struggling to mak
needs were met.

I remember one day finally having a f
versation with God. You know the kind, whe
to Him and tell Him how well you are doing e
and how you can't see why He won't help you
I was really frustrated, and I was running d
sharing with God just how good *I* had been.
I always tithed, I always give anytime I can,
did my best to follow Him in everything He a

Then as I am running down my list, I
"I believe you want me to have a better life fo
ily. I know you don't want us to always stru

I want to encourage you to do your own study in addition to the information I am providing you from God's Word. Allow God to help you gain a better understanding of His will concerning meeting your needs and teach them to your children. The world's system requires that we have resources in order to do anything, and with God's help you can break free from the grip of poverty in the same way that my family and countless other believers have done.

PROOF #1

We Are Redeemed from the Curse of the Law

The first proof that God's will for us is abundance is found in the book of Galatians.

> **Galatians 3:13-14, 29**
>
> Christ has redeemed us from the curse of the law, having become a curse for us (for it is written, "Cursed is everyone who hangs on a tree"),
> 14that the blessing of Abraham might come upon the Gentiles in Christ Jesus, that we might receive the promise of the Spirit through faith.
>
> 29And if you are Christ's, then you are Abraham's seed, and heirs according to the promise.

The Bible tells us in Galatians that Jesus came so that believers could be made free from the curse of the law. What exactly is *the curse of the law*? In order to find out, we need to go back to the Old Testament Levitical Law. The term, "the Law" refers to the first five books of the Bible, or what is known as the Pentateuch. These books are Genesis, Exodus, Leviticus, Numbers, and Deuteronomy.

When we look back through those Old Testament books, we find that the curse for breaking God's law was threefold and included:

- Poverty
- Sickness
- Spiritual Death

There are many people who have the idea that, as believers, we don't have any promise of blessing in this life. I have heard many well-meaning preachers teach that prosperity is a worldly desire and that God does not intend for people to have wealth. Most of what they teach is based on isolated scriptures taken out of context that are typically used to justify their own experience of living in lack. I certainly won't spend time attempting to tear those ministers down. However, I would encourage you to do your own study and refuse to allow your current circumstance (or the circumstances of others) to dictate your theology. The Bible is clear in 1 Timothy 4:8:

> For bodily exercise profits a little, but godliness is profitable for all things, having promise of the life *that now is* and of *that which is to come* (italics mine).

There are blessings and provision that are available to believers both here and in our future!

When we look at the curse found in the Old Testament that is attached to disobedience to God's law, we find that violating spiritual law produces natural consequences.

> **Deuteronomy 28:15-17, 38-40**
>
> But it shall come to pass, if you do not obey the voice of the Lord your God, to observe carefully all His commandments and His statutes which I command you today, that all these curses will come upon you and overtake you: [16]Cursed *shall* you *be* in the city, and cursed *shall* you *be* in the country. [17]Cursed shall be your basket and your kneading bowl.
>
> [38]You shall carry much seed out to the field but gather little in, for the locust shall consume it. [39]You shall plant vineyards and tend *them*, but you shall neither drink *of* the wine nor gather the *grapes*; for the worms shall eat them. [40]You shall have olive trees throughout all your territory, but you shall not anoint *yourself* with the oil; for your olives shall drop off.

These verses show us that the curse of poverty was to come on God's children if they disobeyed God or failed to keep His commandments. As New Testament believers who have received Jesus, we have been redeemed from that curse through the price that He paid. And now because of His sacrifice on our behalf, the blessing of Abraham now belongs to us through our covenant with God. The blessing that God promised to the Old Testament believers included the blessing God gave to Abraham when God said that he was going to cause Abraham to be blessed.

> **Genesis 12:1-3**
>
> Now the LORD had said to Abram: "Get out of your country, from your family and from your father's house, to a land that I will show you. [2]I will make you a great nation; I will bless you and make your name great; And you shall be a blessing. [3]I will bless those who bless you, And I will curse him who curses you; And in you all the families of the earth shall be blessed."

We can see based on a passage in Genesis 13:2, that God did what He had promised: "Abram was very rich in livestock, in silver, and in gold."

God desires those who are in relationship with Him to live in abundant blessing. Notice the word "rich" in Genesis 13:2. The word in Hebrew is *kaved,* and it means heavy, having much, or to be thick. That means Abraham had an abundant supply!

Let's read in the New Testament what the apostle Paul says regarding God's provision in Philippians 4:15-19:

> Now you Philippians know also that in the beginning of the gospel, when I departed from Macedonia, no church shared with me concerning giving and receiving but you only. [16]For even in Thessalonica you sent aid once and again for my necessities. [17]Not that I seek the gift, but I seek the fruit that abounds to your account. [18]Indeed

> I have all and abound. I am full, having received from Epaphroditus the things sent from you, a sweet-smelling aroma, an acceptable sacrifice, well pleasing to God. [19]*And my God shall supply all your need according to His riches in glory by Christ Jesus* (italics mine).

According to Paul when you and I have a need, evidently God will supply all of it! Following God doesn't cost you and me, it always pays.

Let me say this before we go any further. Don't allow the devil to pervert the fact that God wants to provide for your needs. I am not advocating greed and neither is God. But I am saying that for too many years, we have seen the church and God's people living sub-standard in the face of a world set against it. As believers, there should not be any financial hinderance in our lives that would prevent you and I from going and doing anything God calls us to do. We should have an abundance so that we are able to have more than enough to provide for our needs and the needs of others. Trust God to give you twice as much as you need and give away the rest!

- Fund missions
- Care for widows and orphans
- Do good in the name of Jesus

A few years ago, I remember speaking to my father-in-law about a friend of his who was a born-again businessman. The man had so much money, he never had a need he could not provide for. He once gave enough money to a mission work in Africa so that they could buy forty acres at a thousand dollars per acre in order to build a place for orphans to live and be self-sufficient. He made this statement to my father-in-law: "God has blessed me. Why die with a big pile of money and not help anyone?"

Imagine if this man had the idea that many religious people have, that money is the root of all evil. What does the Bible actually say about that? The scripture that many people use to justify living in lack comes from 1 Timothy 6:10 which says:

> For the **love** of money is a root of all *kinds of* evil, for which some have strayed from the faith in their greediness, and pierced themselves through with many sorrows (bold mine).

It is the "love" of money that is the root of all evil. It's alright for you and I to have money. The problem many people face is that they allow money *to have them.*

Again, I am not advocating chasing money or things. If you spend your life chasing money that won't ever lead to true prosperity. If we are following God and adhering to His principles of provision, the scriptures say that Abraham's blessing already belong to us.

- We don't need to covet wealth
- We don't need to chase it.

The abundant provision of God belongs to us as part of the same covenant that says we are saved and that we are healed. Provision is ours to help us reach the world with the gospel of Jesus.

PROOF #2

The Blessing Attached to the Tithe

God specifically outlines several things that happen as a result of tithing one tenth of our income.

Malachi 3:10-12

"Bring all the tithes into the storehouse, that there may be food in My house, and try Me now in this," says the LORD of hosts, "if I will not open for you the windows of heaven and pour out for you such blessing that there will not be room enough to receive it. [11]and I will rebuke the devourer for your sakes, so that he will not destroy the fruit of your ground, nor shall the vine fail to bear fruit for you in the field," says the LORD of hosts; [12]and all nations will call you blessed, for you will be a delightful land," says the LORD of hosts.

In this passage, God says that He will:

- Pour out a blessing bigger than you can hold
- Rebuke the devourer
- Your vine won't cast its fruit (meaning the work of your hand won't fail)
- All nations shall call you blessed (People will recognize that God has blessed you.)

The question needs to be asked then, if God didn't want us to live in abundance, why attach such a blessing to tithing? Additionally, some people have decided that the tithe was just Old Testament law, and therefore we are no longer required to tithe. However, verse 6 in this chapter says, "I Am the Lord, I change not." Since the Bible specifically says that the Lord does not change, we have to believe that in context, He has not changed his mind about the tithe. The reader should also note that Abraham paid tithes to the High Priest Melchizedek five hundred years before the law was even given (Genesis 14:18-20). This means the issue of tithing predates the law.

There are also people who believe that we don't have scripture in the New Testament for tithing. Yet in Hebrews 7:8, the scripture tells us, "Here mortal men receive tithes, but there he *receives them,* **of whom it is witnessed that he lives."** The author of Hebrews is showing us that tithing was practiced by the early church in New Testament worship.

I have tithed all my married life. Additionally, I typically give much more than one tenth of my income and can attest that, over the years, we have seen God honor that commitment. I have also served in pastoral ministry roles in a number of churches throughout the years and find that, nearly without exception, people who argue against tithing are typically not generous with anything—their finances, their time, or any other area of their lives.

If you are looking for reasons to not give generously, you may have answered your own question as to why you struggle to have your needs met. If you will choose to honor God with even the minimum tithe, God will honor you. You truly can't beat God giving! The faithful consistent giving by believers has always helped to contribute to the gospel being preached all over the world, and it is difficult for me to consider ever attempting to find a way to give less to help further the gospel.

In Malachi 3:10, we see that God says we can prove His willingness to provide when we tithe: "Bring all the tithes into the storehouse, that there may be food in My house, And *try Me now in this*." (Italics mine.) Notice also in verse 8 of this chapter what God says about withholding the tithe:

> Will a man rob God? Yet you have robbed Me! But you say, "In what way have we robbed You?" In tithes and offerings.

God has set up the tithe as a means whereby He can bless us. As we give to Him in obedience, we are saying that we trust that He is able to provide for us and we are giving Him the opportunity to rebuke the devourer on our behalf. It is God's will to make sure you and I have our needs met. It was man who needed a savior, and God sent His Son to meet that need. The scripture tells us in Romans 8:32, "He who did not spare His own Son, but delivered Him up for us all, how shall He not with Him also freely give us all things?" God wants to make sure that all of our needs are met!

I recognize that it may sometimes be a struggle to tithe with all of your bills. This is a scenario I know all too well. But I want to encourage you that God will *always* honor His Word and He will *always* make a way for His people. I still remember as situation as a student at Rhema Bible Training College in Broken Arrow, Oklahoma, in the early 2000s. I had come home after receiving my first paycheck from my job at a shipping company and was disappointed by how small my check was. The entire check could not pay even one bill that I owed. I remember standing in my kitchen with my wife and both of us were laughing (I think to keep from crying), and we decided the only thing we could do was give the whole check.

That is exactly what we did. We put the whole thing in the offering the next Sunday. And within thirty days at that same job, I was promoted to the manager of my department!

It had very little to do with the amount of the check, I promise you. Rather, it was our heart to trust

God in the middle of a hard place. I am not telling you to give your whole check to the church, but I am convinced that because I gave that check, God showed Himself faithful to us. God will *always* take care of us if we don't hold back on Him.

God specifically separates tithes and offerings in this passage in Malachi, and I believe that neither of them should be considered as including only our money. The money you have is part of what we can offer to the Lord, but we are not limited by our monetary resources. God will take what we have in our hand, and if you and I release into His service, He can multiply it! (*See* John 6:1-14.)

PROOF #3

The Blessing Attached to Our Giving

In the New Testament, Jesus also promised that our giving would be blessed in abundance:

Luke 6:35-38

But love your enemies, do good, and lend, hoping for nothing in return; and your reward will be great, and you will be sons of the Most High. For He is kind to the unthankful and evil. [36]Therefore be merciful, just as your Father also is merciful.[37]"Judge not, and you shall not be judged. Condemn not, and you shall not be condemned. Forgive, and you will be forgiven. [38]*Give, and it will be given to you: good measure, pressed down, shaken together, and running over will be put into your bosom. For with the same measure that you use, it will be measured back to you* (italics mine).

Jesus said that when we give, it *shall* be given unto us:

- In good measure
- Pressed down
- Shaken together
- Running over

But notice, this scripture is speaking more about the attitude we have towards giving than the amount of the gift we give. We see this same principle of giving in 2 Corinthians 9:6-7:

> But this I say: He who sows sparingly will also reap sparingly, and he who sows bountifully will also reap bountifully. 7So let each one give as he purposes in his heart, not grudgingly or of necessity; for God loves a cheerful giver.

The words *sparingly* and *bountifully* are relative terms. What may seem sparingly for you may be a lot for someone else. The amount we give is less important than the attitude with which we give. Remember the widow in Mark 12:41-44?

> Now Jesus sat opposite the treasury and saw how the people put money into the treasury. And many who were rich put in much. 42Then one poor widow came and threw in two mites, which make a quadrans. 43So He called His disciples to Himself and said to them, "Assuredly, I say to you that this poor widow has put in more than all those who have given to the treasury; 44for they all put in out of their abundance, but she out of her poverty put in all that she had, her whole livelihood."

The Contemporary English Version of 2 Corinthians 9:7 says it this way:

> Each of you must make up your own mind about how much to give. But don't feel sorry that you must give and don't feel that you are forced to give. God loves people who love to give.

Another translation says, "As you determine in your heart or spirit." We must never assume that just writing big checks is the only way to give. As New Testament believers, we should search our hearts and give as the Spirit leads above the tithe (which is ten percent). What you give above the tithe is considered an offering to the Lord.

You and I are to give generously as we are led by God's Spirit. I heard a minister say once that God spoke to his heart and told him to give a particular suit to another minister. This preacher said he had just purchased the suit and was having a hard time letting it go. Instead of giving what God had instructed him in his heart to give, he gave the guy a different suit, and then another, and another, and another until finally, he only had the one suit he knew in his heart he was supposed to give. He eventually gave the suit God asked him to give which left him with none for a while. It is always better to obey God in our giving than to just give large amounts thinking we are impressing God.

You might be giving tithe and offerings instead of sowing your time and talents as the Lord has instructed. But don't think that what God wants you to do will change just because you write another big check!

If God didn't want us to live in abundance, then why would he attach a blessing to our giving in both the Old and New Testaments? Because He *does* want us to be blessed! The only one who doesn't want to see us blessed is Satan, and this is the reason why he fights so hard to keep people convinced that there is no need to give into God's work.

PROOF #4

John's Prayer

The next proof I found in scripture came in the form of a prayer that John prayed when he wrote to his friend Gaius in 3 John. Gaius was one of the members of a church which came under the care of the apostle John. In this epistle, John calls Gaius "beloved" multiple times. It is clear in the writing that John holds a great deal of admiration for this brother. John compliments Gaius for his care for ministers who travel to his area. He is also commended for his faithfulness to both the people he knows and to strangers.

John begins his letter with this prayer for his friend:

> **3 John 1-2**
> The Elder, To the beloved Gaius, whom I love in truth: 2Beloved, I pray that you may prosper in all things and be in health, just as your soul prospers.

I believe it is significant that this prayer and letter are included in the scriptures. All scripture is inspired by the Holy Spirit and notice that in this prayer, he prays that Gaius will prosper and be healthy in the same way that his soul prospers!

A good friend and mentor, Rev. Marvin Yoder, says this in his book *Movin' On Up*, "Your health and prosperity are governed by the condition of your soul. It is impossible for your health or prosperity to exceed the condition of your soul." This means that in order to have the increased capacity for provision, we have to change our thinking about the will of God concerning the subject. If we have the idea that God doesn't want us to have our needs met or we feel like we can't know if He will take care of our material needs, we will never increase our capacity to receive.

Many well-intentioned ministers argue against whether God wants believer's needs met, and if we accept the line of thinking that says God does not want us to experience material abundance, we will always struggle to have our needs met.

Interestingly, I have noticed that some of the loudest voices arguing against God's prosperity are themselves living at a high degree of comfort. They say that they are prosperous because they've worked hard for what they have. That may be true, but if they believe God doesn't want anyone to be prosperous, maybe they need to remedy their prosperity problem by giving all of theirs away.

Third John 2 is dealing with both outward and inward prosperity. If you are questioning God's will to provide for you, then ask yourself, "Would the Holy Spirit inspire John to pray for something that his friend Gaius couldn't have?" If John can pray this way for Gaius, then you and I can pray for people to be blessed as well. I remember another prayer that became popular many years ago. The prayer was so popular, that it even inspired a book that was written called *The Prayer of Jabez*. The Jabez prayer is found in 1 Chronicles 4:9-10

> Now Jabez was more honorable than his brothers, and his mother called his name Jabez, saying, "Because I bore him in pain." [10]And Jabez called on the God of Israel saying, "Oh, that You would bless me indeed, and enlarge my territory, that Your hand would be with me, and that You would keep me from evil, that I may not cause pain!" *So God granted him what he requested* (italics mine).

God will answer any prayer that is in line with His Word. It is for this reason that you and I must read and know the Word of God so that we are praying in line with His will. Another example of God's will for provision is found in the example of Solomon:

> **1 Kings 3:5-13**
>
> At Gibeon the LORD appeared to Solomon in a dream by night; and God said, "Ask! What shall I give you?" [6]And Solomon said: "You have shown great mercy to Your servant David my father, because he walked before You in truth, in righ-

> teousness, and in uprightness of heart with You; You have continued this great kindness for him, and You have given him a son to sit on his throne, as it is this day. [7]Now, O LORD my God, You have made Your servant king instead of my father David, but I am a little child; I do not know how to go out or come in. [8]And Your servant is in the midst of Your people whom You have chosen, a great people, too numerous to be numbered or counted. [9]Therefore give to Your servant an understanding heart to judge Your people, that I may discern between good and evil. For who is able to judge this great people of Yours?" [10]The speech pleased the Lord, that Solomon had asked this thing. [11]Then God said to him: "Because you have asked this thing, and have not asked long life for yourself, nor have asked riches for yourself, nor have asked the life of your enemies, but have asked for yourself understanding to discern justice, [12]behold, I have done according to your words; see, I have given you a wise and understanding heart, so that there has not been anyone like you before you, nor shall any like you arise after you. [13]*And I have also given you what you have not asked: both riches and honor, so that there shall not be anyone like you among the kings all your days*."(Italics mine.)

Notice that God didn't say it was wrong to pray for wealth, and He even went further by telling Solomon that because of his heart to serve, He would give him not just what he had asked for, but also material wealth that Solomon didn't ask for.

Over the years I have had the Lord bless me through the hands of people on a number of occasions including gifts such as a car, a motorcycle, and an expensive watch. I have enjoyed the benefit of these items and then later, I have had the Lord lay on my heart that I was to give some of these items away, which I did. I was pondering these things one day and had this phrase come into my heart. "Son, never ask me for anything you wouldn't be willing to give up for me."

I believe this is a key ingredient to receiving God's blessing in a greater measure. We must keep our heart and motives pure before the Lord. Many times ministers and lay people alike get off track by becoming money minded. If we pursue God and seek first His kingdom, provision will never be a problem. This brings me to my next proof of God's provision.

PROOF #5

Seeking God Produces Abundance

One of the strongest proofs for abundance I found is a very well-known portion of scripture in the New Testament:

Matthew 6:19-33 (KJV)

Lay not up for yourselves treasures upon earth,
where moth and rust doth corrupt, and where
thieves break through and steal: 20But lay up for
yourselves treasures in heaven, where neither
moth nor rust doth corrupt, and where thieves
do not break through nor steal: 21For where your
treasure is, there will your heart be also. 22The
light of the body is the eye: if therefore thine eye
be single, thy whole body shall be full of light.
23But if thine eye be evil, thy whole body shall
be full of darkness. If therefore the light that is
in thee be darkness, how great is that darkness!
24No man can serve two masters: for either he will
hate the one, and love the other; or else he will
hold to the one, and despise the other. Ye can-
not serve God and mammon. 25Therefore I say
unto you, Take no thought for your life, what ye
shall eat, or what ye shall drink; nor yet for your
body, what ye shall put on. Is not the life more

> than meat, and the body than raiment? 26Behold
> the fowls of the air: for they sow not, neither do
> they reap, nor gather into barns; yet your heav-
> enly Father feedeth them. Are ye not much bet-
> ter than they? 27Which of you by taking thought
> can add one cubit unto his stature? 28And why
> take ye thought for raiment? Consider the lilies
> of the field, how they grow; they toil not, neither
> do they spin: 29And yet I say unto you, That even
> Solomon in all his glory was not arrayed like one
> of these. 30Wherefore, if God so clothe the grass
> of the field, which to day is, and to morrow is cast
> into the oven, shall he not much more clothe you,
> O ye of little faith? 31Therefore take no thought,
> saying, What shall we eat? or, What shall we
> drink? or, Wherewithal shall we be clothed? 32(For
> after all these things do the Gentiles seek:) for
> your heavenly Father knoweth that ye have need
> of all these things. 33But seek ye first the king-
> dom of God, and his righteousness; and all these
> things shall be added unto you.

There are people who focus on the portion of scripture at the beginning of this passage in order to build a doctrine against personal or material provision in our lives. They believe we should have nothing on earth, that any wealth we have should only be in the spiritual realm. But this doctrinal position becomes easy to dispute if we read the full context of this chapter.

Jesus is not saying that it is wrong for you to have things. He is showing us that it is wrong for things to have us. Notice He tells us don't take "thought" about these material things. I believe He says it this way because thoughts always precede action. Jesus understood that if we spend all of our time thinking about how to get stuff, pretty soon action would follow, and you and I would be chasing the stuff!

Notice verse 32 says the world *seeks* after these things. The Greek word used in this passage is *epizeteo,* which means to crave intensely. Compare this to the Greek word for *seek* in verse 33 which is *dzayteho,* meaning to worship or desire God. The issue is not the stuff. If we look back at the example of Solomon which Jesus mentions verse 29, and we looked at Solomon's life, we understand that God said he would make Solomon wealthy. Why did Solomon have all of "these things"? Because God saw that his heart was to pursue God, not gold, and when we put God first, He will supply our needs.

There will always be a blessing attached to following God's plans for your life. If you choose to go where God says go and pursue the things God is calling you to, He will make sure that your needs are met. I heard a friend say once that the Lord spoke to his heart and said, "If I ever call you to something, I will pay for it. If you do it on your own, you will pay for it." If we follow God, He will finance the journey!

PROOF #6

The Lord Is Our Provider

I believe that Jesus was the full and final atonement for man's sin. I also believe that the atonement makes provision to meet any need man has in this life and in the life eternal. We read previously:

> **Galatians 3:13-14**
>
> Christ has redeemed us from the curse of the law, having become a curse for us (for it is written, "Cursed *is* everyone who hangs on a tree"), [14]that the blessing of Abraham might come upon the Gentiles in Christ Jesus, that we might receive the promise of the Spirit through faith.

If Jesus redeemed us from the curse of the law, we should want everything that redemption includes. If we look back at the curse found in the law, we find that it included poverty, sickness, and spiritual death (or separation from God). Jesus paid the penalty so that we could be free from the curse of the law and so that Abraham's blessing would be available to us.

We know Jesus paid the penalty for our sin. The scripture says in 2 Corinthians 5:21, "For He made Him who knew no sin *to be* sin for us, that we might become the righteousness of God in Him." We are righteous not of our own merit, but Jesus made us righteous. We can also find that Jesus paid the price for you and I to receive bodily healing. I realize some people do not believe this; however, there is a lot of evidence in scripture that indicates we can receive healing through our redemption in Christ. If you have never been taught this, I would encourage you to study the scriptures for yourself to see what the Bible says.

Sometimes we take the word of others or a personal circumstance of sickness or disease and get the idea that it is somehow not God's will to heal us. We need to recognize that everything that happens is not God's will for our lives. We could say that if everything that happens is His will, then we have perfectly fulfilled the will of God in our lives, and we know that is not true.

The scripture tells us in 2 Peter 3:9 that "it is not God's will that any should perish, but that all should come to repentance." Yet we all know that not everyone receives Jesus, even though that is the will of God. There are certainly some who don't get saved, some who don't get healed, and still some that don't get their needs met. However, these circumstances and situations do not change the Word of God. Let's study and make every effort to be among those who receive God's best!

In the same plan of redemption where Jesus paid for our sins, He also provided for our healing. The Bible tells us in Isaiah 53:5, "But He was wounded for our transgressions, He was bruised for our iniquities: the chastisement of our peace was upon Him; and with His stripes we are healed." There are some people who will claim that this passage refers to spiritual healing. But God does not heal your spirit. When you get born again, you become new, and old things are passed away.

We can see further evidence that this scripture means physical healing when we see the fulfillment of this prophecy:

> **Matthew 8:16-17**
>
> When evening had come, they brought to Him many who were demon-possessed. And He cast out the spirits with a word, and **healed all who were sick,** 17 that it might be fulfilled which was spoken by Isaiah the prophet, saying:
>
> "He Himself took our infirmities and bore *our* sicknesses." (Bold mine.)

Jesus provided salvation at the cross, He provided healing at the cross, and by giving everything He had for you and I, He also provided for our physical needs as well. Jesus redeemed us from the curse of poverty as we see in 2 Corinthians 8:9:

> For you know the grace of our Lord Jesus Christ, that though He was rich, yet for your sakes He became poor, that you through His poverty might become rich.

When we study these words, we can readily see that it includes provision both spiritually and naturally. Jesus gave everything He had so that we could have everything He gave. Of course, we can choose to go through life and reject anything He offers for whatever reason. Although Jesus paid for salvation, we could reject it and die in sin if we chose to, even though it would not be the will of God. As far as that unbeliever would be concerned, what Jesus did would be an empty sacrifice. He might as well not have come (for that person).

We could take this idea a step further. The Bible says Jesus took our sickness the same as he took our sin, but we can choose to reject the sacrifice He made for sickness and die sick. We can then take that same thought another step further and say that although Jesus bore our poverty, we can hear that truth and never accept it for whatever reason and never receive the benefit of the truth. We can accept that he bore our sin and sickness (and live a healthy life and die and go to heaven) but reject that he bore our poverty and die penniless if we choose.

When you and I receive light on a Bible subject we become responsible for walking in the light of it. Once we heard Jesus died for our sins, we became responsible for what we did with that information. In the same way, when we read 2 Corinthians 8:9, we see that

Jesus willingly became poor for our sake. If that's true, we should be willing to receive anything He did on our behalf.

The question regarding the poverty of Jesus is often raised. People will sometimes say that because the Bible tells us in Luke 9:58 that "the son of man has no place to lay His head." that Jesus was poor in His earthly ministry. The reality however is that Jesus did not live in lack while He was here on earth. Whenever Jesus had a need, He always had provision. The scripture tells us that His ministry had a treasurer, that He could feed thousands of people, and that when His taxes were due, He didn't need to take out a loan.

Matthew 17:24-27

When they had come to Capernaum, those who
received the *temple* tax came to Peter and said,
"Does your Teacher not pay the *temple* tax?"
25 He said, "Yes." And when he had come into the
house, Jesus anticipated him, saying, "What do
you think, Simon? From whom do the kings of
the earth take customs or taxes, from their sons
or from strangers?" 26 Peter said to Him, "From
strangers." Jesus said to him, "Then the sons are
free. 27 Nevertheless, lest we offend them, go
to the sea, cast in a hook, and take the fish that
comes up first. And when you have opened its
mouth, you will find a piece of money; take that
and give it to them for Me and you."

Jesus understood that God supplies our need, and that's why He told us to "seek first the kingdom of God."

There is further proof that Jesus was not poor while in ministry found in Matthew 26:6-12:

> And when Jesus was in Bethany at the house of
> Simon the leper, 7 a woman came to Him hav-
> ing an alabaster flask of very costly fragrant oil,
> and she poured *it* on His head as He sat *at the*
> *table.* 8 But when His disciples saw *it,* they were
> indignant, saying, "Why this waste? 9 For this fra-
> grant oil might have been sold for much and given
> to *the* poor." 10 But when Jesus was aware of *it,* He
> said to them, "Why do you trouble the woman?
> For she has done a good work for Me. 11 For you
> have the poor with you always, but Me you do
> not have always. 12 For in pouring this fragrant oil
> on My body, she did *it* for My burial."

Notice Jesus said in verse 11, "For you have the poor with you always, but Me you do not have always." He separates Himself and the poor with this statement. If I make the statement to you that "My wife is out of town, but I am here," there is a separation in our locations indicated. That is what Jesus is doing in this verse.

The poverty Jesus bore on our behalf came just like the bearing of our sins and our sickness. This loss took place as a result of His separation from God. When Jesus was walking in His earthly ministry, He was not separated from God. He said things like, "The Father and I are one," and "If you have seen Me, you have seen the Father." The poverty came for Jesus when he hung on the cross.

The Bible refers to Jesus as the second Adam, and just like the first Adam in Genesis, the loss Jesus experienced on our behalf came as a result of the separation. His poverty began when He was arrested, stripped, beaten, and killed without even a place to be buried. Thank God He is not living in poverty now and because of what He did, we don't have to either.

PROOF #7

It Pays to Follow Jesus

In serving God, I have made a lot of moves over the years. When I first answered the call to ministry the Lord led my wife and I to Broken Arrow, Oklahoma, to attend Rhema Bible Training College. We left there and began pastoring a small church and from there we have traveled to different places serving in different roles in ministry now for nearly twenty years.

I heard a minister say once, "Following God doesn't cost, it pays." I didn't really know what that meant when I first heard it. I always thought that since you were giving up something to follow God, it was sacrificial and therefore, it cost us something. I can see now though, that as I look back over the years, we were blessed and received far more in our obedience than we ever gave up to follow Him.

The principle I am speaking about can be observed in the Word of God concerning the story of the rich young ruler:

Mark 10:17-30

Now as He was going out on the road, one came running, knelt before Him, and asked Him, "Good Teacher, what shall I do that I may inherit eternal life?" [18]So Jesus said to him, "Why do you call Me good? No one *is* good but One, *that is*, God. [19]You know the commandments: 'Do not commit adultery,' 'Do not murder,' 'Do not steal,' 'Do not bear false witness,' 'Do not defraud,' 'Honor your father and your mother.' " [20]And he answered and said to Him, "Teacher, all these things I have kept from my youth." [21]Then Jesus, looking at him, loved him, and said to him, "One thing you lack: Go your way, sell whatever you have and give to the poor, and you will have treasure in heaven; and come, take up the cross, and follow Me." [22]But he was sad at this word, and went away sorrowful, for he had great possessions.

[23]Then Jesus looked around and said to His disciples, "How hard it is for those who have riches to enter the kingdom of God!" [24]And the disciples were astonished at His words. But Jesus answered again and said to them, "Children, how hard it is for those who trust in riches to enter the kingdom of God! [25]It is easier for a camel to go through the eye of a needle than for a rich man to enter the kingdom of God." [26]And they were greatly astonished, saying among themselves, "Who then can be saved?" [27]But Jesus looked at them and said, "With men *it is* impossible, but not with God; for with God all things are possible."

[28]Then Peter began to say to Him, "See, we have left all and followed You." [29]So Jesus answered

> and said, "Assuredly, I say to you, **there is no one**
> **who has left house or brothers or sisters or fa-**
> **ther or mother or wife or children or lands, for**
> **My sake and the gospel's,** 30 **who shall not re-**
> **ceive a hundredfold now in this time—houses**
> **and brothers and sisters and mothers and chil-**
> **dren and lands, with persecutions—and in the**
> **age to come, eternal life."** (Bold mine.)

Many times people tell the story of the rich young ruler and even quote the passage about the eye of the needle to illustrate a relationship with following God that describes a life of being in lack. However, when we read the full context of this story, we see that this is not what Jesus intended to convey. When Peter says to Jesus, "We left all to follow you." Jesus replies that those who follow Him don't lose anything. They actually gain.

The difficulty with earthly blessings is often found in people's unhealthy relationship with things. God doesn't care if you have a motorcycle, a boat, a nice house, or if you go on vacations. The problem arises when these things separate us from following God and His plan for our lives. I am reminded again of what God said to me about stuff years ago: "*Don't ask for anything you wouldn't give up for me.*" This is the key issue that the rich young ruler was facing. He wanted to follow the Lord, but not as much as he wanted to keep his earthly possessions. The young man in this story I believe struggled with an issue that the apostle Paul gave warning about in 1 Timothy 6:17-19:

> Command those who are rich in this present age not to be haughty, nor to trust in uncertain riches but in the living God, who gives us richly all things to enjoy. [18] *Let them* do good, that they be rich in good works, ready to give, willing to share, [19] storing up for themselves a good foundation for the time to come, that they may lay hold on eternal life."

I like how the CEV shares this truth. Verse 17 says:

> Warn the rich people of this world not to be proud or to trust in wealth that is easily lost. Tell them to have faith in God, who is rich and blesses us with everything we need to enjoy life.

Can you have blessings and provision in this life and still make heaven? Jesus said you can! You can ask God to meet needs in your life, you can enjoy God's blessings, but you must always put God's plans and purpose above everything else.

PROOF #8

It Pleases God When We Prosper

The eighth proof that you and I can live a life of abundance comes from the fact that *God is a giver*! I love that statement. It reminds me of how much the Lord loves me. The Bible says in John 3:16, "For God so loved the World, that *He gave....*" It is in God's nature to see that man has a need in His life and then to fill that need for us. There is a scripture in Psalms that I found while seeking the Lord on this subject that really blessed me!

> **Psalm 35:27**
> Let them shout for joy and be glad, Who favor my righteous cause; And let them say continually, "Let the LORD be magnified, Who has pleasure in the prosperity of His servant."

The Good News Translation of this verse says, "He is pleased with the success of His servant." When people don't realize God wants us to be successful, it's because they don't yet understand the giving nature of God. Everything God ever did was to satisfy man's interests. Man was interested in missing hell and going to heaven, so God satisfied that interest. Man needed healing so God satisfied that interest. Man needed peace, man needed to be loved, man needed provision, so God met those interests as well. God is a loving and giving father and what loving, giving father won't take care of His children?

I can remember growing up as the son of a construction worker and a cake decorator. My parents would do everything they could to make sure that my brother and I had our needs meet. My mom would be a single parent for weeks at a time while my dad traveled all over the country looking for work in order to provide for our family. He spent all that time alone on the road, working twelve and fourteen-hour days, because he loved us. How much more will our Heavenly Father provide for our needs because of His love for us.

A number of years ago, the Lord called my wife and me to move to a town in Central Illinois called Mattoon. The former dean of the Bible college I attended was moving there to pioneer a church and when we found out about it, we both felt the Lord was calling us to move to the area and be a help.

It was a struggle at first for us to get in faith about the move. We would be leaving our family, a good job, a church we were pastoring, and we had three young children. In the natural, it seemed like a lot to overcome. We began praying about the move and taking steps in the natural like visiting the area and looking for housing. The main issue was we needed jobs in order to make the move. We continued to pray about the transition and in just a few months we both ended up with good employment opportunities that would help to meet the needs of our family.

The most notable thing about this move was that both my wife and I received positions for employment that had never existed prior to our move. I am convinced that God had supernaturally opened the door for these jobs in order to provide for us as we were following His path for our lives. He is so faithful!

I want you to see something in 1 Timothy 5:8:

> But if anyone does not provide for his own, and especially for those of his household, he has denied the faith and is worse than an unbeliever.

God's Word says here that if you won't provide for your own, you are worse than an unbeliever. I want you to realize that God would not tell us to do something or be something He is not. He wants us to be like He is, and He is a provider. He will always take care of His children!

PROOF #9

We Have the Power for Provision

The Bible tells us in James 1:17 that "every good and perfect gift comes from above." If you and I experience anything noteworthy or good in this life, it is a result of God's love for humanity. As a loving father, He is giving us gifts and talents that can help us prosper and live in abundance here and now. In Deuteronomy 8:18 we read, "And you shall remember the LORD your God, for *it is* He who gives you power to get wealth, that He may establish His covenant which He swore to your fathers, as it is this day."

This passage tells us that God gives us the power or ability to obtain wealth. If He gives us the ability, then it must be His will that we obtain wealth. The question then is for what purpose do we obtain wealth? "That He may establish His covenant which He swore to your fathers." The GNT gives a clearer picture. It says, "He does this because He is still faithful today to the covenant that He made."

It's important to note that it says God gives you

the power to get wealth. It does not say He gives us the wealth, but the *power to obtain it.* How does that power work? To understand that we need to know the definition of this word *power.* In Hebrew, "power" in this scripture is *koach,* and it means several things including vigor, force, capacity, means, ability, might, strength, substance, or wealth. All of these words together comprise the full understanding of having the power to get wealth.

The last word in this definition was wealth, and it may seem strange to say God gives you wealth to get wealth. But it's not really. We have all heard the saying, "It takes money to make money." Everything in God's kingdom begins as a seed. There is a scripture in 2 Corinthians 9:10 that says, "He gives seed to the sower." God will provide seed to help you to reap a harvest in your life. He will also help you by telling you the best place to put that seed. God will provide us with the means and the direction for where to sow our seed, and faithful obedience to His direction will determine the level of our harvest.

God has given every one of us the ability to become prosperous. We don't have to rely on someone else to make us prosperous. We need to ask ourselves what giftings or abilities do I have that if they are developed and used will bring abundance into my life? Living in abundance will require some effort on our part. You and I may have the ability to live in abundance because of God's grace, but that ability must be developed or mined out.

There is an old story that illustrates this point. A man had two sons who believed their father to be very wealthy, and they came to his bedside while he lay dying. The two young men attempted to extract information from their father about where he had hidden his treasure. The old man just kept whispering, "The stump lot. The gold is in the stump lot."

The young men knew which lot their father was talking about. He owned a ten-acre lot that was undeveloped. So after the man's funeral was over, the two sons went to work cutting out stumps and clearing weeds on the lot, looking for the treasure. The young men dug up that whole lot, but they never found anything.

Disappointed, one of the brothers told the other since there was no treasure, they might as well plant the field. The two sons worked hard to finish preparing the soil and planted corn. When the time for fall harvest came, the young men found the gold! It was in those ripe ears of corn that they found their wealth.

That's what it is like for us. We are like that undeveloped lot. With some effort on our part mixed with the ability and the grace God gives to each of us, we find the gold! God has given each of us giftings and abilities that will bring abundance into our lives. If we are going to live in abundance, we are going to have to work to develop those things in our lives.

God will bless what we put our hand to. Deuteronomy 28:8 says, "The LORD will command the blessing on you in your storehouses and in all to which you set your hand, and He will bless you in the land which the LORD your God is giving you." Abundance will never come to our lives by just sitting around doing nothing. If we want anything to flourish, we must put effort into drawing out the potential it contains. Whenever we discover a gifting, talent, or ability in our life, we have to work at it to develop it. Remember that the things God has placed in our lives are the things God can use to prosper us. If we take time to develop our gifts, God will use them to bring abundance into our life.

I hope as you have been reading this that you have taken some notes. I know for me, if I don't write things down, I sometimes fail to put them into practice in my life. If you didn't write notes, don't worry. This is your book so you can always go back and read it again.

We have covered nine proofs that God wants us to live in abundance so far, and I hope they help you as much as they have me. Over the years I have seen that there are more than ten places in the scripture where God proves His desire for us to live a life of abundance. I encourage you to read the Bible and find others.

Here is a list of the proofs we have covered so far along with the main scriptures:

#1 We Are Redeemed from the Curse of the Law (Gal. 3)

#2 The Blessing Attached to the Tithe (Mal. 3)

#3 The Blessing Attached to Our Giving (Luke 6)

#4 John's Prayer (3 John 2)

#5 Seeking God Produces Abundance (Matt. 6)

#6 The Lord Is Our Provider (2 Cor. 8)

#7 It Pays to Follow Jesus (Mark 10)

#8 It Pleases God When We Prosper (Ps. 35)

#9 We Have the Power for Provision (Deut. 8)

Our last one however, for me, is the most compelling proof. It comes to us from the very mouth of Jesus.

PROOF #10

Jesus Came to Give Us Abundant Life

I want to be everything God wants me to be! I think about that sometimes and wonder what it will be like standing before the Lord at the Judgement Seat of Christ. I want to do everything I can to fulfill His plan for my life and I want to experience all He has provided for me.

On that day, I think that there will be lots of things I thought I knew, but in reality my understanding was not to the level I thought. I wonder how much more I will realize that the Lord had in store for me that I never obtained while here on the earth.

This type of thinking makes me all the more determined that when I see something in the Word of God that has been provided for me, I want to experience it in my life. There is a passage of scripture in John 10:10, that I believe really provides a clear picture of God's will for our lives: "The thief does not come except to steal, and to kill, and to destroy. I have come that they may have life, and that they may have *it* more abundantly." Jesus tells us here that He came so that we could have an abundant life! It think it is interesting to note that He distinguishes between life and *abundant* life. Life is good, but Jesus didn't say that He came just so we could have any type of life, He said He came so that we could have an abundant life. He didn't come so we could just barely get by. Jesus came to help us to be the head and not the tail and above and not beneath. (*See* Deuteronomy 28:13.)

I think that this is really good news! You know, that's what the word *gospel* means. The gospel is the good news about what God did for us through Jesus. Jesus said in Luke 4 that He was anointed to preach the gospel, and He gives detail of who the good news was for.

> **Luke 4:17-18**
>
> And He was handed the book of the prophet Isaiah. And when He had opened the book, He found the place where it was written: [18]"The Spirit of the LORD *is* upon Me, Because He has anointed Me To preach the gospel to *the* **poor**; He has sent Me to heal the **brokenhearted,** To proclaim liberty to *the* **captives** And recovery of sight to *the* **blind,** *To* set at liberty those who are **oppressed**." (Bold mine.)

Notice, Jesus included the poor in the list of people He came to preach the gospel to. Satan (the thief) came to steal everything you had, to kill you, and to destroy the plan that God has for your life. But Jesus came to destroy the works of the devil! In 1 John 3:8, we read that "He who sins is of the devil, for the devil has sinned from the beginning. For this purpose, the Son of God was manifested, that He might destroy the works of the devil."

Jesus is the remedy for everything that Satan tries to use to destroy us with, including poverty. As I said earlier in this book, I have experienced poverty in my life. I grew up in a neighborhood that was full of poverty. The town I grew up in was part of the county with the highest poverty level in my state and it was hard to live in that type of lack. I saw people fight over government commodity food because poverty will cause people to grab and take hold of anything they can in order to make it. I saw neighbors become jealous over other people's success because poverty makes you jealous and covetous towards people and things. I have watched as families lived in the same Section 8 housing for three generations and how that housing became dilapidated and even, in some cases, began to separate from the foundation. I have seen parents tell their children no, not because they wanted to, but because they could not afford to say yes.

I am not saying that if you are poor, you are a bad person. I am simply pointing out that the devil will use lack to disrupt the lives of people and that Jesus paid the price for us to experience abundance in order to break the devil's stronghold on people and their communities. I have experienced lack in my own life and in my family and I never want to go back to that feeling.

How do I know it is God's will for us to prosper? Because I do not believe God wants to see people go through the things I have seen, and because if He gave Jesus for us, that means we can have everything we need in order to be free from the curse of poverty. Romans 8:32 asks, "He who did not spare His own Son, but delivered Him up for us all, how shall He not with Him also freely give us all things?"

You and I need to be armed with Bible knowledge in order to make a decision to live in God's abundant provision. If we are confident in God's desire to help us to live abundantly, we will not be moved when the economy is struggling, we won't be limited to a job or our paycheck. We can begin to fully trust that God will always abundantly supply.

Conclusion

There you have it! These ten truths are the things that God showed me from His Word regarding His will for us to live in abundance. I can honestly tell you that finding out about these scriptures and God's will to provide for me have changed my life. I have gone places and done things that a guy with my background was never destined to do.

There are probably some who people who will read this book and say that I am wrong. They might choose to hang on to old ideas or teaching that differs from the things I have shared. There may even be some who label me as a prosperity preacher. However, I honestly don't know one person that has ever said that they wish they would do worse in life. Everyone I know has always seemed to want more. A better crop, a bigger farm, a nicer house, a raise at work, and countless other things. I have been without, and I can't imagine ever wanting to experience lack again.

Why not believe God for more than what you have? Allow God to teach you to experience such an abundance that you can be a greater blessing to your friends and neighbors and to the kingdom of God. Study the scriptures in this book and search out others that can help you see God's desire for you to live in abundance. Let God help you to have such an abundance that you have more than you can use.

I have a family member that is like that, and he is a huge blessing to other people. My father-in-law has always grown a huge garden. He plants more than he can ever eat, and he has more than he can ever put away for the winter. He doesn't grow such a large garden out of greed, he grows it to be a blessing. If he knows you, when harvest time comes, you will always have fresh vegetables. He won't do without, and you won't do without. I believe that's the main reason he always has such a nice garden. God will always cause generous people to have more because he knows he can count on them to help those who haven't yet figured out how His system operates.

I want to encourage you to make a decision that you'll be one of the generous ones. Trust God for abundance and help someone else discover the possibilities that God has for His people. I can share with you that these principles from the Bible have worked for me, and if you don't believe them, you probably won't be bothered with them. If you will take hold of these truths, I can promise you that God has bigger and better in store for you than what you have experienced so far. Trust God and let Him open the windows of heaven and pour out a greater blessing than you can contain.

Do You Know Jesus?

If you don't know Jesus as your Lord and Savior, I want to encourage you to receive Him today. The truth contained in this book is God's way of providing for His children. The amazing thing is that if you receive Him, you can begin to operate in this system of provision, but even more than that, you can become a member of the family of God. God sent Jesus to die for you and me, and His love for us is so deep that Jesus willingly gave His life so that we could be in relationship with God. If you have never made Jesus the Lord and Savior of your life, pray this prayer and start a new life in Christ today.

Dear God,

I come to You in the name of Jesus. I admit that I am not right with You, and I want to be right with You. I ask You to forgive me of all my sins. The Bible says if I confess with my mouth that Jesus is Lord and believe in my heart that God raised Him from the dead, I will be saved (Romans 10:9). I believe with my heart, and I confess with my mouth that Jesus is the Lord and Savior of my life.

Thank You for saving me! In Jesus' name I pray. Amen.

A Message from Rob

Contact Us

ABUNDANCE

Made in the USA
Columbia, SC
19 October 2022

69721771R00046